Giles's War

Dr Tim Benson is Britain's leading authority on political cartoons. He runs The Political Cartoon Gallery and Café which is located near the River Thames in Putney. He is the editor of the annual collection *Britain's Best Political Cartoons*. He has also written numerous books on political cartoonists, including *Churchill in Caricature*, *Low and the Dictators*, *The Cartoon Century: Modern Britain through the Eyes of Its Cartoonists*, *Drawing the Curtain: The Cold War in Cartoons* and *Over the Top: A Cartoon History of Australia at War*.

Giles's War

Cartoons 1939–1945

Edited by Tim Benson

BOOKS

1 3 5 7 9 10 8 6 4 2

Random House Books
20 Vauxhall Bridge Road
London SW1V 2SA

Random House Books is part of the Penguin
Random House group of companies
whose addresses can be found at
global.penguinrandomhouse.com.

First published by Random House
Books in 2017

www.penguin.co.uk

A CIP catalogue record for this book is available
from the British Library.

ISBN 9781847948090

Printed and bound in Italy by L.E.G.O. S.p.A.

Penguin Random House is committed to a
sustainable future for our business, our readers
and our planet. This book is made from Forest
Stewardship Council® certified paper.

No artist captured Britain's indomitable wartime spirit quite like Carl Giles. After the outbreak of the Second World War in 1939, he became known for his charming and irreverent cartoons about life on the Home Front – and his remarkable ability to distil the trials of life during wartime into amusing snapshots of Britain's stiff upper lip. Starting out in 1937 at a small Sunday newspaper, *Reynold's News*, his weekly comics became a source of constant comfort for the British public during blackouts, air-raids and rationing. By the time Giles moved to the *Express* newspaper in 1943, he was well on his way to becoming the country's best-loved cartoonist.

This collection celebrates Giles's work as a young cartoonist forging his reputation during the biggest conflict in global history. During the Blitz, he worked with bombs falling around him – one went through the top floor of the *Reynold's News* building while he was at work there, but luckily did not explode. From 1944 onwards, he saw the final throes of the war first hand, accompanying British forces fighting through Belgium, Holland and then Germany itself, as the official 'War Cartoonist' for the *Express*. He even witnessed the liberation of Bergen-Belsen

**An early Giles cartoon attacking businessmen
who profited from the war effort.**

concentration camp and Germany's surrender to Field Marshall Montgomery at
Lüneburg Heath in 1945. Along the way, Giles's cartoons helped raise a chuckle for
Britons at home and fighting overseas. Spike Milligan, who served in the Royal
Artillery, recalled that 'During the war, Giles's cartoons played no little part in

boosting my morale.' As Lt. Col. Sean Fielding put it in a letter to the *Daily Express* in February 1945, 'Giles, in my opinion (and the soldiers') is the only artist who truly caught the stink, the discomfort and beastliness of the front line.'

Aspects of Giles's wartime career remain obscure, mostly because he disliked his official biographer, Peter Tory. According to Rick Brookes, who later replaced him as cartoonist on the *Daily Express*, Giles was wary of all journalists and avoided interviews and television appearances wherever possible. With Tory, the animosity was mutual: he said that writing Giles's biography was the worst and most boring assignment he had ever been given. At Giles's funeral, as mourners took their seats, Tory remarked: 'People fish in a very small gene pool in Norwich. Have you noticed how they all look like Carl Giles?' Tory wrote that getting Giles to talk about his private life was 'like pushing a ton weight up a steep hill' – this lack of cooperation led to factual inaccuracies and incorrectly annotated illustrations in Tory's biographies of Giles.

Giles's War brings together Giles's wartime cartoons for the first time. It collects over 150 of his earliest drawings for *Reynold's News*, most of which have not seen the light of day since the 1940s. It shows how humour helped keep Britons' spirits up during the darkest moments at home and on the battlefield. And above all, it celebrates the development of a young cartoonist working on an obscure Sunday newspaper into one of Britain's most famous artistic talents – showing how Carl Giles's charming depictions of a nation at war made him a household name by 1945.

✳   ✳   ✳

Giles was born on 29 September 1916, above his father's tobacco shop on City Road in Islington, London – 'well within the sound of Bow Bells,' he later remembered. The second of three children, he came from a line of Norwich farmers on his mother's side, and Newmarket jockeys on his father's: his grandfather had even raced for the Prince of Wales, later Edward VII, in the 1880s. Although he was christened 'Ronald', Giles 'intensely disliked' his first name and dropped it at the first opportunity. Later, when his fellow animators nicknamed him Karlo – because his hairstyle resembled that of the horror film actor Boris Karloff – he soon adopted the shortened version: 'Carl'. The name stuck.

The family tobacco shop was next door to The Angel pub. According to Giles, this was handy for his father, Albert: 'the old man had to pop me somewhere when he went out,' he said in 1944. The boozy spirit of early-twentieth-century London was a recurrent theme in Giles's work. In 1945, the left-wing journalist and Labour MP Tom Driberg wrote that the infant Giles literally 'drank up the earthy, sawdusty, beery atmosphere which [would later] save his art from any trace of unreal aestheticism'. Although Giles remembered City Road being 'a bloody awful dump', he fondly recalled the noise of an eight-line tram junction outside and the 'lovely' smell of the street: 'You got a shower of rain on the dusty streets, and the smells came up like an orchestra, the trams and the oil on the rails and the electricity transformers.' The nostalgic atmosphere of Giles's cartoons owed a great deal to his memories of London. Decades later, he reminisced about his childhood: 'Stew on Monday. Washday. The coal piled up in the outside passage (and watch out if you touched it!). A house full of uncles, cousins, nephews and nieces. Grandfather sitting with his pile of toast by the fire.'

Giles went to his local school, Barnsbury Park. He later drew it as a place for unruly inner-city urchins. His nemesis was a teacher by the name of William James Chalk, who, as 'Mr Chalky', would became one of his most enduring cartoon creations. 'He was a sarcastic bugger,' Giles recalled. 'In his class you weren't allowed to make a sound. Even if you were dying to go to the toilet you couldn't ask. Ooh, he was a cruel man. I vowed to get my own back, and I did.' Chalk left Giles with a permanent dislike of authority in any form, and he spent his entire career ridiculing petty officialdom, be it tax collectors, army officers, traffic wardens, shop stewards and, on the odd occasion, politicians.

He claimed that he was never given a chance in art classes at school. He said his fate was 'to sit under desiccated art masters who made [him] draw that bloody cone, or that wretched green vase which all schools have on the windowsill with never anything in it'. He left school at 14 with no formal qualifications.

Nonetheless, from an early age he loved to draw. When he was four years old he adored the work of Bruce Bairnsfather, who depicted the British Tommies' experiences in the

Mr Chalky

trenches during the First World War. Giles would copy Bairnsfather's cartoons directly from the *Bystander*, which his father regularly brought home. Giles may have inherited his passion for drawing from his father, who had been an amateur artist. According to Giles's sister Eileen, their father loved to paint: 'His subject was always horses, which he did well but he always fell down when he tried to bring people into his pictures. He got hours and hours of pleasure from painting his horses but never did anything professionally.'

By the time he was a teenager, Giles was fascinated by animation, having seen Walt Disney's 1928 short *Steamboat Willie* – the first ever animated cartoon with sound. The film inspired him to get his first job, working at night in an animated cartoon studio on Charing Cross Road cleaning and washing brushes. The job was short-lived. Giles's father wanted his son to become a jockey, as his own father had been, and so he reluctantly began work as a stable hand. But Giles soon disappointed his father by, in his own words, 'going overweight at an early age and sprouting to an impossible stature of five foot ten', which put an end to his horse racing ambitions. It was the last time Giles would have any career outside the world of cartoons.

Giles left the stables in 1930, and after a short stint working as a pavement artist while living with his grandmother in Brighton, he returned to London. He soon got another artistic job – as an office boy making cups of tea for an advertising agency called Superads, which specialised in animated commercials. 'I loved that. I used to walk out to the cinemas, even to Finsbury Park or New Cross, carrying the cans of films, and I used to hold them so that everyone could see the labels. I felt important,' he recalled. He earned the grand sum of ten shillings a week. It was not long before Giles was promoted to be a junior animator and began working on cartoon shorts. Giles later remembered how supportive the other animators were at the beginning of his career: 'The chaps there had more patience with kids than I have,' he said. 'You learn more working alongside other animators than you could possibly learn in art school.' This was his first great opportunity and he took it: 'I never had any formal art training to draw, thank God. I reckon the best bit of apprenticeship I had was drawing funnies for those bloody cartoon films.'

Giles's role at Superads was the first of several animation jobs. In 1934, aged just 18, he went to work in Elstree, Hertfordshire for the director and producer Alexander Korda, who was working on an animation called *The Fox Hunt*. This was to be the first British animated cartoon in technicolour, produced for London Films. It was not a box office success, as Giles later explained: 'Of course, it was a lost cause. Disney was the only thing the public wanted in those days and everything else had to be a straight copy or else it was done for. And I never liked Mickey Mouse as a character!' Giles never held a high opinion of Walt Disney. He referred to him as a 'conman', who was more a showman than an innovator. Giles felt that 'the only way to make film cartoons is to get away from Disney'. He would later turn down a job as an animator for Walt Disney Studios.

Until the mid 1930s, Giles looked set for a career in animated cartoons. But in 1936 he was involved in a serious motorcycle accident that left him blind in one eye and deaf in one ear. He was sent to recuperate at Castle House, Dedham, the Essex home of Sir Alfred Munnings, then President of the Royal Academy, where Giles's uncle worked as a butler. This chance encounter would change the

A model of the carthorse from *Come on Steve!*

course of Giles's career. Munnings gave Giles the closest he would ever have to formal art training. With Munnings's help, Giles used his experience in animation to produce static gag cartoons, some of which were published in *Passing Show* magazine. It was the first step in Giles's transformation from animator into newspaper cartoonist.

Once he was well enough to leave Munnings's house, Giles was recruited to be head animator on a film called *Come on Steve!* about a lumbering, genial old carthorse, based on a 1932 strip by Roland Davies in the *Sunday Express*. But before long, Giles was drawn back to London. In the spring of 1937, his older brother Bert died in an industrial accident while at work in a garment factory. Giles decided to go back to live with his mother Emma, who was now also nursing her ailing husband in Edgware.

Giles's return to London marked a major career shift. As the British animation industry seemed incapable of competing successfully with its American counterpart, he felt he had better prospects as a cartoonist than as an animator. He had long envied newspaper cartoonists: at the age of only 16 he had taken some samples of a comic strip he had devised to the office of *The Times*, with a note asking the Editor to look at the gags he had drawn. Not surprisingly, he did not receive a reply – *The Times* has never had a cartoon strip, and did not even publish political cartoons until the mid 1960s. Once Giles was living back in London in 1937, he speculatively sent some cartoons to newspapers and periodicals. Included was a strip cartoon about the exploits of a boy called Young Ernie.

After rejections from magazines including the *Illustrated Carpenter and Builder*, Giles got his first big break when he received a belated reply from Bernard Boothroyd, the Humour Editor of the left-wing Sunday newspaper *Reynold's News*. It was published by the Co-operative Press, which through the Co-operative Party had strong ties with the Labour movement. It was known for being the only newspaper to oppose the 1938 Munich agreement. *Reynold's News* did not employ a regular cartoonist, but published four single-panel gag cartoons from foreign cartoonists around the world entitled *The State of the Foreign Market*. Boothroyd, seeing the makings of a popular cartoonist in Giles, replied on 17 September 1937. 'I am sorry I have retained your drawings for so long,' he wrote, 'but I like the style of

**Giles's first cartoon for *Reynold's News*, published
with the caption 'Someone ought to tell 'im!'**

them and kept hoping I might find space for some of them. I think some of them are genuinely funny, and would like to use them.'

Boothroyd suggested that if Giles could re-draw some of the cartoons he had submitted, *Reynold's* would publish them. One cartoon, of knight with sock-suspenders (see above), was retained by Boothroyd 'in order to experiment with it – to see if I can reproduce it in a limited space'. It was published a week later on 26 September 1937. From then on, Giles became a regular contributor to the paper. By December, *Reynold's News* was so impressed with Giles that three days before Christmas, the Managing Editor, Sydney Elliott, offered him a full-time contract. This stipulated that Giles was to 'prepare drawings for Page Two; to prepare a weekly Comic Strip under Mr. Boothroyd's direction; and to undertake such general work, like the preparation of maps, as may be required by the editorial staff' – and all at a weekly salary of six pounds six shillings. The *Young Ernie* strip appeared for the first time on 9 January 1938. Elliott advised Giles that the strip 'should bear neither labels nor caption; if the joke was not obvious without the aid of a written explanation, it was no joke'. Giles accepted the challenge, and the cartoon was a hit. 'Needless to say, Ernie was Giles himself,' Elliott pointed out: 'The little fellow mocking misfortune and poking fun at the pompous fools who delight in pushing other people around.'

Giles worked from an easel in the *Reynold's News* library. According to Elliott, the area around Giles's work-space was soon 'a child's delight and a newspaper cashier's nightmare; a litter of the latest models of the airplanes, motor cars, speed boats and trains which were the stock-in-trade of his cartoons'. One fellow staffer, Gordon Schaffer, remembered how Giles 'enjoyed working on his cartoons. He would do a bit – draw a character – then stand back and say, with a huge grin on his face: "Look at that silly bugger there." We didn't know of course how famous he was going to be.' Giles usually worked between six and ten hours on a cartoon so that he could draw elaborate details and authentic settings. According to the journalist and historian James Dugan, his genius as a cartoonist was due to the training he had received as an animator:

The secret of Giles's dramatic cartoons lies in his movie training. He draws in a panel shaped like the movie screen; his carefully built

**The first ever appearance of Giles's character Grandma,
in *Our Time* magazine in September 1940.**

background architecture is as authentic as a naturalistic stage set-
ting; his characters are placed on stage with directorial skill. When
he shows his drawings to friends he delights in telling what the characters have been doing up to the moment he has chosen to draw
them and what happens to them afterward. In dreaming up a cartoon situation, he imagines a complete dramatic sequence and orders

his brain children to act it out. When they come to the climactic moment, Giles says mentally, 'Hold it!'

Giles's earliest cartoons at *Reynold's News* already contained the energy and wit that would make him famous. His childhood admiration for Bruce Bairnsfather came through in his early wartime work, as did his longstanding admiration for Graham Laidler, who worked under the pseudonym 'Pont'. When Laidler died in 1940 at only 40 years old, Giles said he felt 'the same sort of shock as when someone dies in the family. I missed his drawings and went on missing them.' In Giles's early work for *Reynold's News* one can also see a similar curvy line to that used by Laidler's fellow *Punch* contributor, Fougasse, as well as the minimalist wispy approach used by the American *New Yorker* cartoonist James Thurber. Giles later called his wartime work 'primitive' compared to what came after, and at times this was certainly true. However, towards the end of the war one can see that he had already honed his skills as an accomplished draughtsman.

✳   ✳   ✳

Until the war broke out on 3 September 1939, Giles generally drew joke cartoons, illustrations for Boothroyd's regular column, 'Yaffle', and the *Young Ernie* strip. He drew only a handful of political cartoons. But once the country was at war, he tried to find the funny side to international politics, especially by making fun of Hitler and Mussolini. In March 1940 he received his call-up papers, but was found unfit for military service because he was partially sighted. Keen to assist in any way he

A photo of Giles on his wedding day, surrounded by his Home Guard regiment.

Giles's wedding as depicted in that week's *Young Ernie*.

could, he joined his local Home Guard unit on Edgware Road, which was attached to the Middlesex Regiment; his experiences there provided him with plenty of material for his cartoons throughout the war. It was this gift for finding the humorous side to life on the Home Front that would make Giles famous.

The early years of the war were a happy time for Giles. On his morning commute on the Northern Line to the *Reynold's* office in Kings Cross, he would frequently bump into his first cousin, Joan Clarke, as she commuted from Hampstead to her job as a typist at the *News Chronicle*. According to Giles, the pair had known each other 'since she was that corny old gleam in her father's eye'. They soon started courting, and were married in March 1942 at a ceremony in East Finchley. At the wedding, Giles's Home Guard colleagues lined up outside the church using their bayonets to give him a guard of honour – a scene he depicted in a *Young Ernie* strip the following week. The marriage drew Giles even further into the world of London newspapers: Joan's father was the circulation manager for the *Evening News*.

The pair were devoted to each other. Giles relied on his wife for the rest of their life together – and not just romantically. His sister Eileen once said that 'Giles would be completely lost without her . . . She runs their home and business side of his life with great efficiency.' As Giles put it after the war, 'She's my secretary, nursemaid and everything else thrown in. I'm always trying to catch her out when we go on a trip, but she's never forgotten anything yet.' Only after his death did his colleagues reveal that Giles also had a long-term mistress: according to cartoonist Raymond 'JAK' Jackson, the *Daily Express* would pay for him to visit a secret lover at the Savoy Hotel whenever he was in London.

Giles also made lifelong friends while at *Reynold's News*. A committed socialist, Giles felt comfortable at a left-wing publication, and even considered joining the Communist Party in the late 1930s. 'The only thing that my father left me was a very true saying appertaining to politicians,' Giles once remarked: '"the further the monkey climbs up the tree, the clearer you can see his arsehole."' He shared *Reynold's News's* opposition to the then Prime Minister, Neville Chamberlain, and his policy of Appeasement. In Giles's eyes, the Prime Minister had been totally discredited: 'Anyone with a ha'porth of sense knew that you couldn't like Chamberlain.' His antipathy towards the political establishment would stay with him through his life: he once said he 'love[d] drawing cartoons of politicians, especially if you can make them look as ridiculous as possible'. Although he later moved to the Conservative-backing *Express*, Giles would remain left-wing until he died. In 1966 he described himself as a 'dirty leftist' and a 'Bentley-driving socialist' – 'but I'm still enough of a socialist to wish that everyone could drive one,' he added. He would later say that he 'detested' the right-wing politics of his *Express* colleague Michael Cummings, and refused to have any of his cartoons on display in his Suffolk home or studio. Over the years, Giles grew tired of being asked if his wealth had affected his political outlook: 'I'm always getting asked how I reconcile my Socialist views with my money, you know?'

Their shared politics made Giles's colleagues at *Reynold's* – notably Alan Hutt, Gordon Schaffer and Monty Slater – great drinking buddies. Every day they went to local pubs along Gray's Inn Road, including the Pindar of Wakefield, the King's Head and – Giles's favourite – The Bell. The only colleague Giles did not get on with was the News Editor, Arnold Russell: 'I hated the bloody sight of him,' he said later:

He was a typical Tory fart, typifying the little capitalist shit that Alan, Gordon and Monty would warn us all about. He was difficult as a News Editor, too. Bad tempered, always firing off at everything. We all knew him as the terror of Richmond Gulch. In his first week in the Home Guard he had been posted to a lonely vigil as a sentry in Richmond Graveyard. I did a cartoon of him looking miserable as sin, surrounded by tombstones.

Giles wrote several articles for *Reynold's News* and never missed an opportunity to have a dig at Russell. In one article, he wrote, 'I have to put up with interruptions from the News Editor, who keeps dropping his funny little jokes at my expense, and every time he makes one of these little jokes everybody laughs "Ha, Ha." So of course, I have to laugh "Ha, Ha" as well.' Giles would later blame Russell for his decision to leave the newspaper.

By 1941, Giles felt that he had outgrown *Reynold's News*. His reputation as a cartoonist was growing both in Fleet Street and across the country, despite his publication's relatively small circulation. His cartoons were being syndicated in other newspapers, and *Reynold's* was inundated with requests from readers to publish an annual anthology of his cartoons; one reader suggested that this would be the perfect Christmas gift to send to troops serving overseas.

Arnold Russell, news editor at *Reynold's News*.

An increasingly ambitious Giles started to think about a bigger audience than the one he had, as well as greater remuneration and more space for his work in the newspaper – something *Reynold's News* could not offer him.

He approached Bill Farrar, an editor at the Labour-controlled *Daily Herald*, to ask for a job. Farrer had been looking for another cartoonist to work alongside George Whitelaw, who had joined the newspaper in 1938. Giles even got as far as negotiating a contract for himself of £1,200 a year, four times what he was currently earning. However, the deal fell through when the Editorial Director of the *Daily Herald*, John Dunbar, rejected Giles on the grounds that he felt his caricature was so poor it was not possible to know who was who in his cartoons. In a letter to Giles, Farrer reported that Dunbar 'thought you could not draw faces – that your Hitlers would not be identifiable. There's a page for your memoirs!' Farrer had a point: Giles later admitted to a colleague that he 'couldn't draw people', and for this reason he never attempted to be a political cartoonist.

By the spring of 1943, Giles was busier than he had ever been and was beginning to feel the strain. Apart from his duties for *Reynold's News*, he had taken up animation work for the Ministry of Information from his small Ipswich studio, near his new marital home in Tuddenham, Suffolk, with six animators to assist him. One of the commissions was a three-minute animated cartoon designed to increase grenade production. The grenade, known then as a Mills bomb, is the hero of the film. It is at first cocky, then overawed by the far grander weapons of war, but finally does its job by devastating the German eagle. Ministry of Information officials were so impressed with it they began to refer to Giles as the 'Cockney Disney'

Giles (back left) with a group of cartoonists including 'Vicky' (back row, third left), 'Strube' (front left) and David Low (front row, second left), meeting the Minister of Food, Lord Woolton.

and asked him to make another film on how to instruct expectant mothers in pre-natal care. Unfortunately, British mothers never got to find out: the film was never made. Giles's storyboard was declared highly unsuitable. His central character was an unborn child who loafed around inside his mother smoking a cigar and giving out prenatal advice in a voice highly reminiscent of the American comedian W.C. Fields. Giles also produced cartoons for several other Ministries, including Defence, Health, Food and Agriculture and the Railway Executive Committee. When the Home Guard asked Giles to design backcloths and posters for an event in June 1943, he replied that he was working 12 to 14 hours a day for the Ministry so would be unable to do it.

The overwhelming workload made Giles even keener to move on from *Reynold's News*. In September 1942, Giles's friend Sydney Elliott had left *Reynold's* to work for the *Evening Standard*, owned by Lord Beaverbook. For Giles, working at one of Beaverbook's papers seemed increasingly appealing: although Beaverbook was a Tory peer, who later admitted to using his newspapers primarily for propaganda purposes, he had a long history of employing left-wingers on his publications. A 28-year-old Michael Foot had just replaced another radical left-winger, Frank Owen, as Editor of the *Evening Standard*: the two of them had written the classic anti-appeasement polemic *Guilty Men*, under the pseudonym 'Cato'. The *Standard*, encouraged by Beaverbrook, also supported the popular left-wing cause for an early Second Front in Europe. This was meant to take pressure off the Soviet Union, which was bearing the brunt of the fighting against the Germans.

Beaverbook's *Evening Standard* also employed the most talked-about cartoonist of the time, David Low. Beaverbrook had given Low a much-lauded contract that made him the first cartoonist to have 'complete freedom in the selection and treatment of his subject matter in his cartoons'. Giles was a great admirer of Low and later described him as 'by far the greatest of our political cartoonists'. Giles must have looked on enviously at the cartoonists employed by Beaverbrook. Not only were Beaverbrook's cartoonists the best paid men in Fleet Street, they were also given an unprecedented amount of space in the paper for their cartoons. Low received a half page for his daily cartoon in the *Evening Standard* and a full page for his collection of topical cartoons on a Saturday.

On 18 July 1943, Giles decided enough was enough. He contacted his former boss, Sydney Elliott, about the possibility of being employed by the *Evening Standard*. Elliott told Giles there was no vacancy for a cartoonist, but that there might be an opening at another Beaverbrook paper, the *Express*. Despite his left-wing views, Giles found the Tory-backing *Express* appealing. He later said he saw the *Express* as 'a kind of Palladium, a vast stage that had room for everyone'. Elliott introduced him to John Gordon, Editor of the *Sunday Express*, who Giles then contacted to discuss becoming an *Express* cartoonist.

Giles was lucky in his timing. There had been no vacancy either at the *Daily* or *Sunday Express*: Sidney Strube had been the staff cartoonist on both papers since 1912. However, Arthur Christiansen, Editor of the *Daily Express*, had just fallen out with Strube over his lack of support for the 'Second Front Now' campaign. According to Strube, Christiansen was obsessed with commissioning cartoons about the Second Front. Strube refused: 'The people were not in that mood . . . I suggested [a different] idea but of course he wouldn't look at it. He was furious and walked up and down his room saying I'll get you on the Second Front yet! Next day, he was at it again. I still refused to do his idea. He said I didn't believe in the Second Front. I replied that I did but that we were not yet ready to launch one.'

Christiansen never forgave Strube for standing his ground. From that moment on he was determined to replace Strube with a cartoonist more in line with his own ideas and views. Yet he could not sack Strube, who was enormously popular with readers and still had the support of Lord Beaverbrook. Christiansen had once consulted Beaverbrook about an idea of Strube's that was not in line with the *Express*'s opinions; Beaverbrook had said that Strube was 'a law unto himself'. Instead, Christiansen decided to make life difficult for Strube in the expectation that it would lead to his resignation. He told Strube that he was going to employ another cartoonist to work alongside him because he needed plenty of time to train somebody in preparation for Strube's eventual retirement. Strube told Christiansen that he would be unhappy if another cartoonist 'appeared on my pitch – after all my loyalty to the paper it would hardly be fair'. He pointed out that at 50 years old he did not consider himself an old man and was certainly not ready to contemplate retirement. 'If Churchill had retired at 50,' he told Christiansen, 'we would probably have already lost the war!' Undeterred, Christiansen informed Strube that he was no longer to be the sole cartoonist on the paper: from October 1943, he would be joined by Carl Giles – a cartoonist Strube thought of as little more than another amateurish joke artist.

Giles was contracted to draw two cartoons a week for the *Daily Express* and one for the *Sunday Express*. He was allowed to work from his new marital home in Tuddenham. This was not altogether unusual. David Low had already set the

**Giles in his studio at home at
Hillbrow Farm, Suffolk.**

precedent by working from his own studio in Hampstead, free from editorial control or proprietorial influence. Giles, too, was free to draw what he liked and did not have to seek approval for any of his ideas.

Although Beaverbrook eventually came to love Giles's cartoons, at first he was disappointed. He might have been under the misapprehension that Giles was, like Low and Strube, a political cartoonist. Arthur Christiansen tried to correct this in a letter to Beaverbrook:

In one of your notes you say that Giles is not developing as you had hoped, and that he has not got the 'firm, stern, harsh qualities of Low'. I do not think that Giles could possibly compete in Low's field. He is not a political cartoonist. Whenever he tries this line of country, he flops badly. But his humour makes the widest appeal in this country, and there is no sign whatsoever of his losing his grip on the public.

In Giles's defence, he had never said that he was a political cartoonist. He saw his cartoons as social satire meant solely to entertain, and he was distrustful of any attempt to analyse his work. According to Robert Allen, in his history of the *Daily Express*, Giles had imposed upon himself a rule that 'he never draws a cartoon which is primarily political . . . He has never believed that politics on its own makes good journalism. He points out that if politics sold papers, then the *Morning Star* [the newspaper of the Communist Party], which has yet to discover jokes, would be the best-selling paper in the country.'

Giles either felt guilty about resigning from *Reynold's News* or was made to feel so by his former colleagues, who believed he had sold his soul to the Tories. This reaction hurt him deeply. Once he had left, he wrote to Boothroyd in order to defend what Giles himself described as a 'Judas's act'. 'I left *Reynold's* as you may well imagine in the face of violent opposition and took the risk of losing the friendship of many people for whom I have a great respect, and who I believe had come to look on me as a permanent fixture of *Reynold's*,' he wrote: 'Foremost, yourself.' The reason was 'that I felt like a complete change of stage and scenery. Many times during the past few years one or other of the Nationals have invited me to work for them and I have declined, but this time I went because I did not, at a future time, want to look back and say, "I wish I had, etc."' He also insisted he had not jumped ship for the money. 'It was not the financial side which influenced me in any way as things have been running fairly smoothly in that way lately owing to the fact that I am working on film production for the Ministry of Information, and a multiplying of salaries did not interest me greatly, which I hope eliminates the "pieces of silver" side of the story,' he told Boothroyd.

After he moved to the *Express*, Giles tried to create a smokescreen so that he couldn't be accused of betraying his former colleagues. He said that he had turned down offers from rival newspapers over the past years out of loyalty to *Reynold's News*. What's more, he fed a rumour that the *Reynold's* News Editor, Arnold Russell, had repeatedly cut down the size of his cartoons. According to his colleague, Gordon Schaffer, Russell 'wanted to squeeze some more news into the page. As a result he demanded that Giles's cartoon be cut down. He was furious. I think, though I cannot be certain, that this is what triggered him [Giles leaving]. In practice, this did not just simply mean that the cartoon was reduced in size but on occasions parts of it were cut out, which meant losing a section of the drawing.' In his biography of Giles, Peter Tory wrote that 'this represented to the artist an act not just of insensitivity but also brutal barbarism'. In fact, none of Giles's cartoons was ever reduced in size or cut into at *Reynold's News* – but Giles was happy to let the rumour spread.

Giles also insinuated that the *Express* had made him an offer he couldn't refuse. 'They bribed me,' he said. 'They stuck a cigar in my face and told me what was to be.' He persuaded his editor John Gordon to make out that he had been extremely reluctant to leave *Reynold's News*. Gordon, in his introduction to Giles's first published collection of cartoons in 1946, said he had taken 'the lid off Aladdin's cave and let him [Giles] peep in' – in other words, Gordon had offered him a King's ransom. Gordon wrote that Giles had replied, 'I am very happy where I am. I would be very unhappy if I changed,' and that he had 'required a considerable amount of persuasion before he would move to the *Express*'. This was simply not the case: Giles had explicitly approached Gordon for a job and not the other way around.

Giles's desertion of *Reynold's News* was met with sadness by its readers. One Giles fan sent in a poem about his departure entitled 'Why oh why?':

Laski and Driberg, Brailsford and Bullett,
Excellent writers with differing styles,
We read them with profit, enjoyment and fervour,
But tell me, oh why have you robbed us of Giles?
The serious side of your paper is splendid,
Historical truth is stored in your files,
Each Sunday for years you have brightened the day for us,
Now it's all different – page two has no Giles.
Letters from readers raise serious issues,
Young Ernie would light up our faces with smiles,
Dear Editor, you cannot know, I am certain,
The difference it makes to us not to have Giles.

Giles's first cartoon for the *Sunday Express* was published on 3 October 1943 and was on a grand scale. It offered a smorgasbord of characters: Hitler, Mussolini, Goebbels and Goering, all seated in the Reich Chancellery, surrounded by Stalin and numerous Soviet soldiers. It was an ambitious start. He settled in quickly at the *Express*, inspired by the knowledge that he now had a much larger audience. However, a number of readers were unhappy that Strube had been partly usurped by the introduction of a 'lesser' cartoonist and wrote to the Editor to complain. One said, 'I have been a reader of the *Daily Express* for many years. I am a great admirer of Strube and wonder why he is being coupled with an inferior cartoonist. I have mentioned the subject to a number of *D.E.* readers who are also surprised. Is anything now good enough for us?' Another reader complained: 'I am rather surprised to find another cartoonist introduced into your paper. How I like Strube. He is miles in front of any other cartoonist and should not in my opinion, and many others, be paired with an inferior artist!'

Despite the criticism, Giles was enjoying his new job. He liked living in Ipswich, finding it comfier – and safer – than life in war-torn London. It also improved his work, as Sydney Elliott noticed: 'Giles finds recreation in wandering around the market-place at Ipswich. He goes there and to the nursery and the pub for his characters and types and gags.' He also took his inspiration from a nearby American air base. Stationed there were members of an engineering battalion, most of them African-Americans. Their task was to build runways from which American bombers could take off. Giles shared a love of jazz with many members of the battalion, and soon became their friend and local champion. He was horrified

Giles's drawing of Ike, an American GI he played jazz with.

by the racist attitudes of the white GIs, who refused to socialise with their black colleagues.

On Saturday evenings the engineers would cycle to The Fountain Inn. In April 1944, a *Vogue* journalist visited to write a feature about Giles, reporting the scene from his local pub: the African-American soldiers would arrive balancing 'bass fiddles, drums, trumpets, trombones and saxophones and their other instruments on the handlebars. The bass player would lean his instrument at a 60-degree angle to keep clear of the low ceiling, with its Scotch thistles, Tudor roses, and fleurs-de-lis impressed there by Elizabethan workmen. The Suffolk farmers would then crowd into the back room with their pints of mild and bitter as Giles struck up the opening bars on the piano and the 16-piece hot band went into "Big Fat Mama With the Meat Shakin' on Her Bones".' And the renowned photographer Lee Miller captured that exact scene in a picture that accompanied the *Vogue* article.

*　*　*

By 1944, Giles was becoming unsatisfied with depicting the war from across the Channel – he wanted to witness it first-hand. After the successful invasion of northern France in June 1944, Giles was keen to experience life at the Front. He joked that with a name as Germanic as 'Carl', he 'had to join the Army . . . or else I'd have been lynched!' He asked Christiansen if he could go over as a war correspondent. At first it was considered too dangerous to risk sending him, but in September 1944 Giles was given his War Correspondent's licence, along with the rank of Captain, with orders to proceed by military aircraft to Brussels to represent the *Daily Express* with the 2nd Army. The *Express* also gave him an enormous pay hike – increasing his salary four-fold to a whopping £3,900 per annum. As he prepared to leave for Holland, Giles witnessed what he thought was the 'most glorious sight' of the war: the Allied air armada going out over East Anglia towards Arnhem as part of the invasion of occupied Holland. He admitted at that moment to being 'a jingo-ist'. Three days later, he was in the battle itself.

Giles travelled to Belgium in a Dakota, his first ever flight. Once there, he noticed British soldiers grumbling more about the awful weather conditions than about the enemy itself: 'There are many things to be said of this Holland and its Nijmegens, Eindhovens, and the rest of the front line towns and villages. I doubt if the average soldier's comments would get past even the most broadminded censor, but one and all agree that: (a) It is cold. (b) It is wet. (c) There may be worse places. (d) But not many. In fact, what beats most of us around these parts is why the Germans, having been pushed nearer home, are trying so hard to come back again.' He came to loathe any Belgians who collaborated with the Nazis: 'I'd like to shoot 'em straight out,' he said at the time. 'My conscience would be clear after three or four drinks.'

Giles had to wear a full military uniform while he was on the battlefield. What he found most disconcerting about it was not the itchy woollen battledress but having to wear 'WC' – for 'War Correspondent' – in white letters on his helmet. 'Can you imagine anything so daft?' he remarked. Giles complained about it to his superiors in case people got the wrong impression about what it stood for. Eventually, orders came back from London that the 'W' could be removed. 'After that I was required to go round just wearing the letter "C",' he said. 'Daft buggers!'

Within days of arriving, Giles was driven to the front line near Eindhoven. This was where he witnessed the fighting for the first time. 'The noise was unbeliev-able,' he recalled. 'Shattering. At first all you wanted to do was dodge in and out of doorways, like in the Blitz but a bloody sight worse . . . Bullets seemed to be coming from every direction, which I suppose they were. The last thing that came naturally to mind was to set up an easel, get out the pencils and start drawing amusing cartoons.' But as the 2nd Army fought its way from Belgium towards Germany, Giles began to send back 'amusing' sketches for readers of the *Express.* Perhaps his most enduring creation from this time was a new stock of characters for his cartoons after the war: the famous 'Giles family': 'I first conceived the idea and main character when I was a war correspondent, actually, and the whole thing just ballooned from there,' he reported later.

In April 1945, Giles was with the Coldstream Guards when they liberated Bergen-Belsen concentration camp in northern Germany. 'You could actually hear the screams and the shouting, from what I suppose you would call the depot, where a train full of prisoners had just drawn in. All you could do was look and just try to absorb what you were seeing,' he said. Initially, Giles did not want to enter the camp at all, but a colleague from the *Daily Express* told him, 'You have to go in, Carl. We both have to. It is important that we see it so that we can pass it on . . . When you see this in the papers back home you won't want to believe it, any more than will the readers. We have to confirm to them that this place existed.' Giles entered the camp and was horrified. The *Express* had asked him to draw in full what he witnessed there, but Giles could not bring himself to. Instead, he drew the various rooms and cells – and not the thousands of dead bodies that littered the ground.

Giles even met the camp commandant, Josef Kramer. He was disconcerted when Kramer said he admired his drawings. Kramer gave Giles his Walther P38 pistol and holster, a ceremonial dagger and his swastika armband. In return he asked for a signed original cartoon. 'I have to say that I quite liked the man. I am ashamed to say such a thing,' Giles later wrote. 'But had I not been able to see what was happening outside the window I would have said he was very civilised. Odd, isn't it? But maybe there was a rather dishonourable reason. I have always found it difficult to dislike someone who was an admirer of my work.' Giles never sent Kramer a signed original: 'What was the point? He had been hanged.' Ultimately he gave Kramer's pistol and armband, as well as the whip carried by SS Guard Irma Grese, warden of the women's section of Bergen-Belsen, to a private collector in Suffolk. The scenes he saw at Bergen-Belsen stayed with him for the rest of his life. In 1992, he said that 'Not a day or night goes by even now when I don't think of Belsen.'

Giles remained with the 2nd Army until the very end of the fighting, even witnessing the German surrender at Lüneburg Heath in May 1945. As the war came to an end, he couldn't help but feel ambivalent. When Mussolini was executed in April 1945, he admitted to feeling a strange sense of loss: 'I sure hated to see old Musso go. He was half my bloody stock in trade.' The end of the Second World War marked the end of one of the most innovative periods in Giles's career.

* * *

By the end of the war, Lord Beaverbrook had been won round to Giles's cartoons. He wrote to him to praise his work: 'It is with pride and joy that I look at your work in the *SE* and also in the *DE* . . . everybody admires and praises your work . . . Yesterday Sir Sholto Douglas [the Marshal of the Royal Air Force] was speaking in praise of you, and he said that in the desperate days of the Battle, he always followed your appearance in the papers.'

In Giles's view, the war had transformed the way the British public thought about cartoonists. He felt that before the war they had not been, in his words, 'cartoon conscious'. In an article Giles wrote in June 1945 entitled 'How It Looks to the Cartoonist', he said: 'I think the war has made people more alive to situations and environments. I know this by the large number of interesting letters I receive from people nowadays, especially men in the Forces. Sometimes a man will write saying he likes or does not like such and such a cartoon, and then go on to give an interesting and intelligent reason why. This seldom happened before the war.'

Giles also thought that during the war, the cartoon came into its own as a propaganda tool. 'Besides being merely a means of giving a laugh, the cartoon, particularly during recent years, has become a powerful weapon,' he wrote. 'By ridicule you can sometimes bring to light a situation quickly and effectively in its correct proportion. Take that Musso. (For whom let all cartoonists be truly grateful.) We know there was nothing really funny about him or any other Fascist or Nazi, but I am sure that one thing that pompous little gent could not stand was ridicule. By causing people to laugh at such a creature, I think a cartoon fired a good shot at making them realise in a cheerful way the futility and stupidness of Fascism.'

By 1945, Giles's cartoons were being seen by millions of people every day. In the course of seven years, he had gone from being an obscure artist drawing for a tiny left-wing newspaper to working for the biggest publication in the country. His success would continue to grow: in post-war Britain, Giles became an institution. Each year his annuals topped the bestseller lists at Christmas time, and he stayed with the *Express* for a staggering 48 years – a record that is only surpassed by Sir John Tenniel and Sir Bernard Partridge at *Punch*.

Only in the late 1980s did Giles begin to consider retiring. In his seventies, his failing health and eyesight led to deterioration in the quality of his output: he left the *Daily Express* in 1989, and was encouraged to leave the *Sunday Express* in 1991 – a year before his long-time colleague, Michael Cummings, was fired. In some ways, however, Giles remained young to the end. His sub-editor Alan Frame recalled that in the 1990s he 'was still driving his Bentley Turbo and took his mistress in it when they stayed at The Savoy'.

By the time he died in 1995, Giles had established himself as the most popular cartoonist in Britain. The comedian Tommy Cooper once said that 'Giles is the funniest cartoonist in the world. He makes me, like millions of others, laugh out loud.' The artist Graham Sutherland commented that Giles gave him 'more pleasure than any other cartoonist. I think he is a great draughtsman, and his insight into the curious goings on of human nature is phenomenal.' And in 1999, he was voted the British public's favourite cartoonist of the twentieth century.

He also had an enormous influence on his fellow cartoonists. Ronald Searle, creator of *St Trinian's*, claimed no one could touch Giles 'in his superb understanding of human behaviour', while the *Mirror*'s 'Vicky' described him as 'a present-day Hogarth'. Generations of artist would emulate his style: he inspired Leo Baxendale to create the 'Bash Street Kids' for the *Beano*, and 'Mac' and 'Chrys' of the *Daily Mail* both emulated Giles's approach in their cartoons. *Guardian* cartoonist Steve Bell once said, 'The wonderful thing about Giles is that he offered a wealth of observation.' In later life Giles even came to resent his level of influence: the *Evening Standard*'s 'JAK' adopted such a similar aesthetic that Giles worried that he was trying to steal his job.

Yet if Giles was the quintessential cartoonist of post-war Britain, the style he became renowned for was forged in the struggles of the Second World War. The features that made Giles's characters distinctive – the bemusement at people in positions of power; the sense of humour in the most trying situations; the stoicism in the face of adversity – were characteristics that Giles had seen, and drawn, during the war. In 1945, reflecting on the importance of cartoons during wartime, he said, 'Perhaps the most important thing the cartoon gives is a balance. It's a relief after reading the heavy and serious matter to be able to turn to your cartoon, which, as long as you like it, and you laugh, is a good one, however bad!' Over the next four decades, it was this outlook that made Giles one of Britain's greatest ever cartoonists.

The Cartoons

Young Ernie

In 1938, as war with Germany began to seem ever more likely, the British government created giant, hydrogen-filled 'barrage balloons', designed to defend towns and cities in southern England from low-flying enemy aircraft.

23 January 1938 — *Reynold's News*

Hitler's Birthday Card

The Prime Minister, Neville Chamberlain, turned 70 on 18 March 1939. Three days earlier, Hitler's forces had marched into Czechoslovakia. It now became clear that Hitler could not be trusted and that Chamberlain's policy of appeasement had failed. Giles's cartoon is a parody of one by Bernard Partridge (see below). The original cartoon was inspired by a notorious letter published by the *Daily Mail* four days before the 1924 General Election, which had attempted to undermine Labour Prime Minister Ramsay MacDonald by linking him with a Communist leader, Grigory Zinoviev.

19 March 1939 — *Reynold's News*

The Office Air Raid Rehearsal –

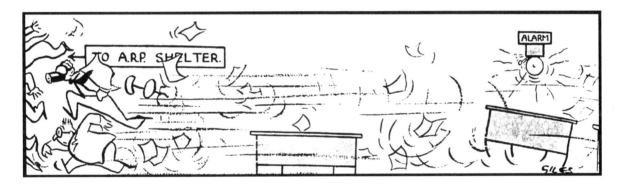

– And The Real Thing

As early as July 1939, public information leaflets were warning the British public of the need for greater discipline during air raid rehearsals at work.

20 August 1939 — *Reynold's News*

**'Will honourable English gentleman
please to accept their tlowsers?'**

Because *Reynold's News* was a morning newspaper, the 3 September issue was printed too early to include coverage of the major news story of the day: Britain's declaration of war on Germany. Giles's cartoon deals with a dispute with Japan over British settlements in China that had ended in diplomatic humiliation for Britain.

3 September 1939 — *Reynold's News*

'Oh, Boy! Oh, Boy!! Oh, BOY!!!'

A typically irreverent cartoon involving Hitler, Hermann Göring, Joseph
Goebbels and an RAF fighter plane.

8 October 1939 — *Reynold's News*

'He says he can hear a rattle or something.'

British tanks were initially deemed slow and vulnerable, and were often unreliable.

15 October 1939 — *Reynold's News*

'Booh!'

By November 1939, over 38 million gas masks had been issued in Britain.

19 November 1939 — *Reynold's News*

'Sorry to interrupt – but I've called about your dog-licence!'

In December 1939, 160,000 members of the British Expeditionary Force arrived in France.

3 December 1939 — *Reynold's News*

'Morning, wiseguys. Have you heard anything of the *Graf Spee* lately?'

Two days earlier the German battleship *Graf Spee* had been badly damaged by British warships. She was to be scuttled by its captain on 17 December to prevent her falling into Allied hands.

'. . . and here's a picture of my brother Fred when he was six!'

17 December 1939 — *Reynold's News*

'. . . this is my own, my native land.'

From September 1938, women were invited to join the British Army to serve in non-combat roles.

4 February 1940 — *Reynold's News*

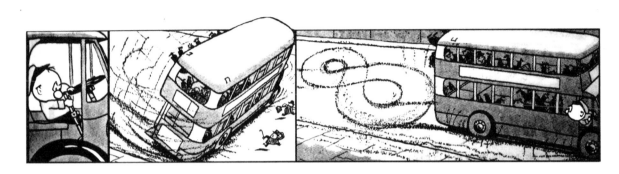

Young Ernie

On 11 February 1941, Giles followed up this cartoon with a note in *Reynold's News* saying that a 'reader from Manchester' had been in touch. '*Dear Mr Giles – Allow me to point out that your last week's cartoon of Young Ernie is absurd. There is no road in England wide enough for an omnibus to do a figure eight*,' said the letter. 'You see?' Giles lamented. 'You just can't get away with it.'

4 February 1940 — *Reynold's News*

Up in the Clouds: 'Dear Mum, I'm sorry to hear Willie's got measles and that Uncle George fell down stairs but didn't hurt himself much . . .'

18 February 1940 — *Reynold's News*

'Please can we have our ball back?'

Allied soldiers faced off Nazi troops on the Franco–German border prior to the full-scale German invasion of 1940.

25 February 1940 — *Reynold's News*

'For the last time Madam, this is not the Baby Linen Counter!'

17 March 1940 — *Reynold's News*

'Tch! Tch! – There She Goes Again!'

Shown here is a German siege gun called the *Schwerer Gustav*. With a weight of 1,350 tonnes, it was the heaviest mobile artillery ever built.

21 April 1940 — *Reynold's News*

'Blimey – so I 'ave!'

'Ah! Here you are, Major. I want you to meet Lil . . .'

12 May 1940 — *Reynold's News*

'A pity der vind, it changed, mine Reverence.'

This cartoon was published nine days after German paratroopers invaded The Hague. The assault was one of the first parachute assaults of the war, and ended in failure for the Nazis.

19 May 1940 — *Reynold's News*

'Do you like your eggs done three or four minutes, sir?'

26 May 1940 — *Reynold's News*

Leopold Looks On

German forces invaded the Low Countries on 10 May 1940. On 28 May, after 18 days of continuous German bombardment, King Leopold III of Belgium unconditionally surrendered. This cartoon appeared alongside a wistful Robert Louis Stevenson quote: 'The world is full of a number of things, I'm sure we should all be as happy as kings.'

Young Ernie

Between 26 May and 4 June, the British Expeditionary Force was evacuated from Dunkirk in northern France.

9 June 1940 — *Reynold's News*

**'I like this bit, Musso. They refer to you here
as "this five-foot-six waddling tin-pan Caesar".'**

The Italian leader Benito Mussolini declared war on France and Great Britain on 10 June. 'First they were too cowardly to take part,' Hitler remarked. 'Now they are in a hurry so that they can share in the spoils.'

In mid-1940, fears of an invasion of German paratroopers were at their height. With most young men conscripted into the military, the government called on those remaining in Britain to join the Local Defence Volunteers – later renamed the Home Guard.

30 June 1940 — *Reynold's News*

**'Well, one of you mob will have to take on this
triumphal march into London, anyway!'**

By 1940, rumours were circulating that Hitler had employed a gang of
body-doubles for protection.

14 July 1940 — *Reynold's News*

'I think I'm speaking for everyone, Grandpa, when
I ask you to quit singing "Run, Rabbit, Run"!'

The comedy duo Flanagan and Allen had a hit with the song 'Run, Rabbit, Run' after
they changed its lyrics to poke fun at the Luftwaffe.

11 August 1940 — *Reynold's News*

'O.K. Buddies. Reach for the ceiling. This is a stick-up.'

Young Ernie

The Battle of Britain had begun in June. Britain's victory owed a great deal to radar, which had been developed in the mid-1930s to help the RAF detect incoming planes.

18 August 1940 — *Reynold's News*

'All I said to the Sergeant was: "What couldn't you do to a nice pint?"'

The East African campaign started in August 1940 when Italian forces attacked the British colony of Somaliland.

'When you can spare a minute, Boss, there's someone here to see you.'

On the day this cartoon was published, RAF Fighter Command claimed victory in the Battle of Britain after the Luftwaffe's largest bombing attack yet was repelled.

15 September 1940 — *Reynold's News*

Young Ernie

'O.K., Fred! Run and tell the C.O. we've got an invasion or something.'

Throughout 1940 there were growing fears of a German invasion.

22 September 1940 — *Reynold's News*

'Now stir the fire, and close the shutters fast,
Let fall the curtains, wheel the sofa round.
So let us welcome peaceful evening in.'
— William Cowper, 'The Winter Evening'

September 1940 marked the start of the Blitz. Britons became used to improvising air-raid shelters under stairs and in doorways.

Throughout 1940 there were fears that German paratroopers would be dropped into England ahead of a general invasion.

'At a wild guess, Herr Gomm, I would say we are arriving at Whipsnade.'

6 October 1940 — *Reynold's News*

'I suppose you wouldn't like a wash, polish and grease while you're here?'

13 October 1940 — *Reynold's News*

**'That makes us quits for the damn great hole
they made in my garden.'**

In the summer of 1940, the RAF had
stepped up its bombing campaign
against German cities.

20 October 1940 — *Reynold's News*

Winston Churchill, who had assumed the premiership in May 1940, put up a sign in the Cabinet War Room that read, 'Please understand there is no depression in this house and we are not interested in the possibilities of defeat – they do not exist.'

10 November 1940 — *Reynold's News*

Young Ernie

10 November 1940 — *Reynold's News*

**'His Lordship's remarks could be quite interesting
when he sees this little lot, Cooper.'**

17 November 1940 — *Reynold's News*

'Don't worry, Uncle George. It isn't loaded.'

1 December 1940 — *Reynold's News*

'Two small lemonades, please.'

A characteristic example of Blitz gallows humour.

8 December 1940 — *Reynold's News*

In fact, recent historical research on the Battle of Britain has revealed that it was British pilots who were forced to rely on the Germans' search and rescue operation in the Channel, and not the other way round.

15 December 1940 — *Reynold's News*

'Some people they hav-a da vera strange sense-a da humour.'

In the previous month, Royal Navy biplanes had largely destroyed the Italian fleet at the Battle of Taranto in Southern Italy.

22 December 1940 — *Reynold's News*

Roof Spotting. The 2 a.m. Feeling

'Roof spotters' were stationed on top of buildings in towns and cities to watch out for approaching enemy bombers.

29 December 1940 — *Reynold's News*

'And now we will ask Mr. Murphy to play the third movement of
Brahms' Concerto No. 2 in B Flat Major, Opus 83.'

'All right, all right. You carry on. You'll soon find out WHY it's silly to sit there.'

26 January 1941 — *Reynold's News*

'Suppose we pull this lot for speeding?'

Between December 1940 and February 1941, the British military forced the Italian Army's 'Blackshirts' to retreat all the way from Egypt to Libya's northern coast.

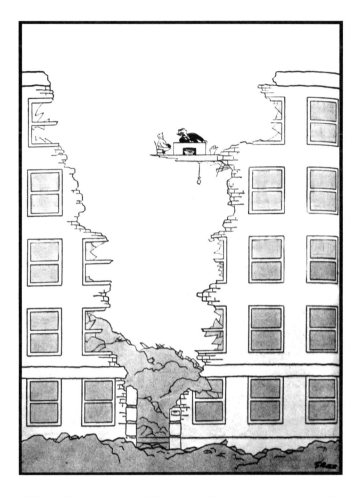

'What d'you mean: ONLY one of his nuisance raids!!'

Hitler's 'nuisance raids' attacked strategically unimportant sites in an attempt to demoralise civilians.

23 February 1941 — *Reynold's News*

'Gentlemen – when this war is over we must see that it is absolutely impossible for there to be any danger of *another* peace.'

Giles's newspaper often criticised arms dealers and businessmen who were thought to be profiting from the war effort.

2 March 1941 — *Reynold's News*

Young Ernie

2 March 1941 — *Reynold's News*

'Vot you mean – you don't think you know nodding about it!'

Resistance in the Nazi-occupied Netherlands tended to involve acts of small-scale sabotage – hiding refugees, distributing leaflets and cutting railway lines.

16 March 1941 — *Reynold's News*

Young Ernie

London Underground stations served as makeshift air-raid shelters during the Blitz.

30 March 1941 — *Reynold's News*

'Who are these rough men, Wilfred?'

Military Police (MP) officers were famous for their no-nonsense approach
to keeping conscripts in check.

20 April 1941 — *Reynold's News*

'Now I want you boys to go in and win.'

27 April 1941 — *Reynold's News*

**'Sieg Heil! Got it I 'aff! Suppose we tell everybody we've
never even heard of anybody called Hess?'**

A week previously, Rudolf Hess, once Hitler's right-hand man, had fled
Germany and parachuted into Scotland in an attempt to broker peace. His
plan had come unstuck when he was intercepted by a pitchfork-wielding
farmer and handed over to the police. The man shown speaking is Joseph
Goebbels, the Nazi Minister for Propaganda.

'What you doing in the Derby, Cyril?'

25 May 1941 — *Reynold's News*

Tea in the Garden

'Well, well, well. Whatever will they be up to next?'

Australian soldiers played a central role in the Allied invasion of Syria.

15 June 1941 — *Reynold's News*

Young Ernie

The Home Guard painted over place names on British road signs in an attempt to disorientate any invading German soldiers.

'Himmel! Dey toss der coin for vich vun gif us der vorks!'

Germany invaded its former ally Russia on 22 June 1941.

29 June 1941 — *Reynold's News*

The Blacksmiths of Minsk

According to the caption in *Reynold's News*, 'When three German tanks entered Pinsk and stopped because of lack of petrol, Russian Guerrillas climbed on top of the tanks and put their machine-guns out of action with hammers. Then blacksmiths appeared and began [to] dismantle the tanks and the bewildered Germans surrendered.'

3 August 1941 — *Reynold's News*

**'Where do you suppose our dear Fuehrer picks up
this story about a pack of phoney peasants?'**

Having occupied Eastern Europe, German forces met unexpectedly strong
resistance when they reached Smolensk.

10 August 1941 — *Reynold's News*

'Take no notice, Mr. Ferguson. It's probably a gag of some kind.'

17 August 1941 — *Reynold's News*

'I'll give you 'Ome Guard!

31 August 1941 — *Reynold's News*

Young Ernie

31 August 1941 — *Reynold's News*

'At least he doesn't have a blasted sergeant bawling at him all day long.'

7 September 1941 — *Reynold's News*

The man who spoiled Caesar's audience

Giles frequently poked fun at the pomp of fascist states – in this case, the Nazis' appropriation of the Roman salute.

14 September 1941 — *Reynold's News*

'His argument is that as a taxpayer he has as much
right to inspect things as anybody else.'

5 October 1941 — *Reynold's News*

'You wait till you've been billeted in this ---* place for a few months.'

Having fended off Italy's attempted conquest of Egypt, British troops stationed in North Africa now had to defend against an invasion by the German military.

12 October 1941 — *Reynold's News*

'This is the SECOND time this week you've only brought down three Heinkels!'

By 1942, thanks to the development of advanced new anti-aircraft ships, the Royal Navy had become adept at shooting down German Heinkel bombers.

2 November 1941 — *Reynold's News*

'And when you come to think that Hitler reckons
the Germans are the superior human race–.'

'And where would you be if Parliament hadn't passed
the Declaration of Rights in 1689?'

16 November 1941 — *Reynold's News*

'Lions in Libya? Who ever heard of lions in Libya!'

Under pressure from the British Eighth Army, German forces continued their retreat into western Libya.

30 November 1941 — *Reynold's News*

'So you sent your luggage in advance, Private Abercrombie?'

This cartoon appeared on 7 December 1941, that day that Japan launched a surprise raid on the American naval base at Pearl Harbor, bringing the USA into the war. *Reynold's News* went to press too early to include news of the attack.

7 December 1941 — *Reynold's News*

'I've asked him. He says he ain't.'

14 December 1941 — *Reynold's News*

Young Ernie

4 January 1942 — *Reynold's News*

'Corporal – Take these things out of here!'

By the end of 1941, Allied forces had defeated the Italian military in East Africa.

11 January 1942 — *Reynold's News*

'Who said this fellow hibernated for the winter?'

The Soviet counter-offensive forced exhausted Nazi troops to retreat 150 miles from Moscow. One of the few surviving photos of Giles from his time at *Reynold's News* shows him drawing this cartoon.

11 January 1942 — *Reynold's News*

'Nasty weather we're having, Ivan.'

18 January 1942 — *Reynold's News*

Hitler had expected a quick victory against the Soviet Union, so Nazi troops had not been supplied with winter clothing. As the Russian winter set in, German forces began to suffer frostbite and many froze to death.

'This is nothing Tovarishch. You should have seen the one that got away.'

By early 1942, Soviet forces had captured 120,000 German prisoners of war.

25 January 1942 — *Reynold's News*

'During the past months the Russians have violated all the international laws of civilised warfare and have committed acts of unimaginable foulness.' – Joseph Goebbels

By now groups of Soviet partisans were regularly harassing German forces in Eastern Europe.

15 February 1942 — *Reynold's News*

'Good Evening, Sir Lancelot.'

With most of Britain's weapons dispatched overseas, the Home Guard was left to improvise an arsenal from outdated guns and spears.

1 March 1942 — *Reynold's News*

'Don't let this fancy Cossack stuff get you down. I've seen it all before in circuses.'

Most of the Red Army's motorised regiments had been destroyed in the German invasion. In response, the USSR created several new horseback infantry units.

8 March 1942 — *Reynold's News*

'Weddin'? I ain't 'eard nothin' about no weddin'.'

According to the caption in *Reynold's News*, 'Although we doubt very much if Giles was wearing a gray topper at the time, he was nevertheless married at Finchley yesterday to Miss Joan Clarke, who we understand, he has known since she was age 0. He refused to tell us either the time or the place in time for us to procure a picture of what is to him a happy if somewhat terrifying event.'

15 March 1942 — *Reynold's News*

'I'm afraid you're going to find me a rather difficult person to jog along with, and perhaps a little intolerant, Sergeant-Major.'

29 March 1942 — *Reynold's News*

'Come, gentle Spring! ethereal Mildness! come . . .'
– 'The Seasons' by James Thomson

The German army began to fight back against the Soviet counter-offensive, but was undermined by Russia's notoriously muddy spring weather.

5 April 1942 — *Reynold's News*

'I want you men to imagine the enemy are approaching in large numbers,
supported by tanks, flamethrowers, paratroops, etc. etc. . . . '

A gentle dig at the Home Guard.

12 April 1942 — *Reynold's News*

'Trust Sahibs please to excuse violation of honourable game.'

Japanese forces had invaded the British colony of Burma in March 1942.

17 May 1942 — *Reynold's News*

'Personally, Fred, I think they're making a great mistake by having insufficient covering fire on their right flank.'

7 June 1942 — *Reynold's News*

'Don't it make you wish you was one of them real soldiers, Fred?'

An affectionate dig at the British Army's non-combatant units, which played no role in attacking and capturing Axis troops.

14 June 1942 — *Reynold's News*

Young Ernie

"'Urry along there – war workers.'

Women of all social classes were expected to get behind the war effort.

21 June 1942 — *Reynold's News*

'Don't be selfish, Ivan. This one is for our little Anna.'

28 June 1942 — *Reynold's News*

'Two and six a shift raise, look mun. They'll be paying us wages next.'

Miners were given occasional pay rises during the war, but continued
to object to the lack of a minimum wage.

12 July 1942 — *Reynold's News*

**'I remember the time when it was the *chauffeur* who
had to wait outside while the *officer* had his hair cut.'**

Chauffeuring for army officers was one of the most popular roles taken on
by women as part of the war effort.

19 July 1942 — *Reynold's News*

'And remember, my Luftwaffe Lovelies, no peeping.'

In July 1942, British forces in Libya had taken 7,000 German
and Italian soldiers prisoner.

2 August 1942 — *Reynold's News*

'Now 'oo got the best bargain?'

Five thousand women were conscripted into the Post Office in 1942.

'O, Venice is a fine city . . .'

Joseph Goebbels, who was responsible for the Reich's propaganda films, visited the Venice Film Festival in September 1942.

6 September 1942 — *Reynold's News*

'How many more times must I tell you to shut der door ven ve submerge?'

**'Headquarters on the phone, George. Colonel says that
number eight battery you got 'im last week's a dud.'**

By the summer of 1942, the Japanese Army had overwhelmed the British forces stationed in Burma.

　　　　　4 October 1942 — *Reynold's News*

'Look out, Basil. 'Ere comes the Mikado.'

18 October 1942 — *Reynold's News*

'Hold tight, boys. 'Ere comes that dangerous criminal
wot missed a couple of 'Ome Guard parades.'

23 October 1942 — *Reynold's News*

'I've got spurs that jingle, jangle, jingle . . .'

Britain's traditionalist cavalry officers were ridiculed for continuing to wear spurs on their boots, despite horses having been phased out. The cartoonist David Low wrote that he created his most famous character, Colonel Blimp, after reading an army officer's letter to a newspaper that insisted that it was essential to wear spurs inside tanks.

1 November 1942 — *Reynold's News*

'Remember that bit about the tall dark man
in your 'oroscope, Spike? Well, 'ere 'e is.'

8 November 1942 — *Reynold's News*

'Op it, some of yer. I ain't capturing more than a 'undred at a time.'

The Second Battle of El Alamein in November 1942 ended with defeat for German and Italian forces in North Africa. According to the caption in *Reynold's News*, 'Axis troops are rushing to give themselves up.'

15 November 1942 — *Reynold's News*

'Dunkirk – pah! Ven id comes to der real retreat id is our glorious sons off der farderland 'oo vill show der vorld 'ow id is done.'

22 November 1942 — *Reynold's News*

'Come, Mr Brown. Let's hear you say in a loud clear voice:
"Move over to the right there, please!"'

29 November 1942 — *Reynold's News*

'It's none of my business, comrade, but you're running in the wrong direction.'

Through the winter of 1942–3, Russian and German forces were in a bloody stalemate on the Eastern Front.

6 December 1942 — *Reynold's News*

'Yoicks! Sez you!'

US soldiers caused a stir when they were first stationed in England in 1942. Under the headline 'Americans Take Jeep to the Hunt', *Reynold's News* accompanied this cartoon with a news story: 'US troops were somewhat surprised last week when a magnificent stag bounded across their range with a US Army Jeep hard on its heels, also bounding. The local hunt followed, making a poor second.'

13 December 1942 — *Reynold's News*

'Confound you, sir! Every time I mention New World Planning I don't expect you to chime in with your "'Oos New World Planning?"'

The war was far from over, but by 1943 Britons were already discussing what kind of country they wanted to build after Germany was defeated – and in whose interests it should be governed.

3 January 1943 — *Reynold's News*

'Beef-eaters? We ain't beef-eaters. We live on Spam like everyone else.'

American GIs had to get used to the British rationing system, which was even more stringent than that of the US.

'I let you drive – and what happens?'

17 January 1943 — *Reynold's News*

'Something wrong here, Boss – according to the Russian communique they only wiped out 12,000 on Thursday. I make it 12,000 and two.'

German forces in Stalingrad finally surrendered in early 1943. The battle, which left over 700,000 Axis troops dead, was the turning point in the Allies' favour on the Eastern Front.

24 January 1943 — *Reynold's News*

'How about me and you girls nipping down to the seaside for the afternoon?'

7 February 1943 — *Reynold's News*

'And what do they call you – "Snow White"?'

The German Navy lost 244 U-Boats in 1943 – three times their losses in the previous year.

'Don't bother to address the envelopes.'

21 February 1943 — *Reynold's News*

The land girl's first morning.

Agricultural workers in the Women's Land Army – known as 'land girls' –
shocked many country-folk by working the fields while the men were at war.

28 February 1943 — *Reynold's News*

'No 'e aint – 'ee's a captin.'

14 March 1943 — *Reynold's News*

'Sergeant – I'm going to pretend I haven't seen something I think I've just seen.'

21 March 1943 — *Reynold's News*

'I said blast 'em and their manoeuvres – that's what I said.'

The Home Guard's mock battles sometimes caused disruption in Britain's villages.

28 March 1943 — *Reynold's News*

'Now you mention it – I DID think those plans looked a bit odd.'

4 April 1943 — *Reynold's News*

'What's 'e think we are, -----*! commandos?'

18 April 1943 — *Reynold's News*

'How you like-a this to tella da people? Now that we 'av achieved our purpose in Somaliland, Eritrea, Abyssinia, Cyrenaica, Tripolitania, and Tunisia, I promise you it will not take-a me very long to think up where we can take a run from 'ere.'

The remnants of Mussolini's forces in North Africa surrendered to the Allies on 13 May 1943.

16 May 1943 — *Reynold's News*

'Emma – You remember them seeds of yourn you put in yesterday behind the tree? Well I've got a feeling they ain't going to come to much this year.'

3 May 1943 — *Reynold's News*

'The correct term, Private Wilson, when referring to a Commanding Officer
is 'C.O.' Not "there goes the toffee-nosed old basket."'

Renowned British artists were commissioned to design posters and artworks for the Ministry of Information.

6 June 1943 — *Reynold's News*

'It doesn't take much to collect a crowd in London these days.'

This cartoon appeared just over a month before Mussolini was dismissed from office and arrested.

'Of course, old man, you will appreciate that all
I am telling you is most frightfully secret . . .'

20 June 1943 — *Reynold's News*

'Oh Romeo, Romeo! wherefore art thou Romeo?

By 1943, British railwaymen had become used to working side by side with women.

27 June 1943 — *Reynold's News*

'Cyril – 'av you 'ad my nail-file?'

4 July 1943 — *Reynold's News*

'There is nothing, absolutely nothing – absolutely nothing – half so much worth doing as simply messing about in boats.' – *The Wind in the Willows*

More German U-boats were sunk in July 1943 than in any other month of the war.

After the defeat of Axis forces in North Africa, the Grand Council of the Italian government passed a vote of no confidence in Mussolini on 25 July 1943. He was arrested and imprisoned the same day.

1 August 1943 — *Reynold's News*

'They've sent a better batch this time, Mr. Jenkins – only two of them are under six.'

With coal stocks running low, the government began to conscript young men aged 18–25 to work in the mines.

8 August 1943 — *Reynold's News*

'Is my honourable friend aware that someone has been playing the bloody fool?'

By the summer of 1943, there were growing calls to open a second front in France.

22 August 1943 — *Reynold's News*

'Now 'and over 'alf a dozen of them clothing coupons you got under there.'

In 1943, the clothing ration was reduced to 36 points per person –
enough to buy only three dresses or two coats in an entire year.

12 September 1943 — *Reynold's News*

'Since you figure on giving him a come-back it's a pity we've been referring to all Italians as a bunch of spaghetti-eaters for the last few weeks.'

This was Giles's last cartoon for *Reynold's News*. It appeared a week after German paratroopers rescued Mussolini from captivity by raiding the Italian prison that was detaining him. Later that month, he was installed as leader of a north Italian puppet state.

19 September 1943 — *Reynold's News*

'Hermann – you've left that verdammt door open again.'

This cartoon was Giles's first work for the *Express* newspapers, published just after the Red Army struck a major blow to the Germans on the Eastern Front.

3 October 1943 — *Sunday Express*

Secret Weapon

This cartoon – featuring Mussolini, Goebbels and Göring – came amid rumours that the Nazis had developed a devastating secret weapon. It was Giles's first work for the *Daily Express*.

17 November 1943 — *Daily Express*

'Git up them stairs!'

By the end of 1943, the tide was turning against the Axis powers. Stalin, Churchill and Roosevelt met in Tehran to coordinate their military strategy against Germany and Japan.

12 December 1943 — *Sunday Express*

'Someone's rocking my U-Boat . . .'

November 1943 was another bad month for the German Navy. Eighteen U-Boats were sunk by Allied forces. 'Someone's Rocking My Dreamboat' had been a hit song the previous year.

14 December 1943 — *Reynold's News*

'Lay that pistol down, Mama . . .'

Giles was fond of referencing contemporary pop music – in this case 'Pistol Packin' Mama', a 1943 country hit which tells the story of an adulterous man who is shot by his jealous girlfriend.

16 December 1943 — *Daily Express*

'The Fuehrer wishes me to say how happy he is to think that, when the enemy invade, he can rely on the whole-hearted support of you – the working people of Europe . . .'

As the war entered its penultimate year, resistance movements in German-occupied territories grew. The French Resistance alone claimed 100,000 members.

25 January 1944 — *Daily Express*

**'These damn Japs are showing us all up – we shall
have to think up a few new ones.'**

By 1944, the brutality of the Japanese Army was well known. On 2 February the Foreign Secretary confirmed that Britain and the US intended to prosecute Japanese war criminals when the conflict ended.

3 February 1944 — *Daily Express*

'This Montgomery ain't the only one who's fed up.'

Bernard Montgomery, one of Britain's most senior military officers, was disgruntled that he had missed out on leading the Allied invasion of France: the job had gone to an American, the future president Dwight Eisenhower.

10 February 1944 — *Daily Express*

'Never mind about it not being 'arf wot we're giving them – let's git 'ome.'

In January 1944, the Luftwaffe began a new bombing campaign over Britain which became known as the 'Baby Blitz'. From 20 February onwards, the Allies struck back with an enormous bombing campaign nicknamed 'Big Week'. The *Sunday Express* owner, Lord Beaverbrook, contacted the newspaper's editor by telegram 'to say how much he enjoyed' this cartoon.

27 February 1944 — *Sunday Express*

'All right – have it your way. I *still* say that I thought we had already been occupied by Germany for years.'

Having given orders to occupy Hungary on 12 March, Hitler now devised a plan for the conquest of Romania. The half-tone sky in this cartoon caused problems for the *Express*'s editor because of the wartime shortage of quality paper. Two days after publication he wrote to Giles, 'Your cartoon on Rumania was OK, but you must not give me so much solid background while our paper is so thin and of such poor quality. If I had published the whole of your cartoon last night, page 1 would have been obliterated!'

26 March 1944 — *Sunday Express*

'I suppose this wretched ban on the coast means another holiday at home.'

Allied troops were sent to the coast as plans for the invasion of France got underway. In April, the British government banned civilians from going within ten miles of the southern and eastern shorelines.

5 April 1944 — *Daily Express*

'Morning General. What's all this we see in the papers last week about wolfram?'

Although Spain was officially neutral, its fascist government had been supplying the Nazis with wolfram (tungsten), the metal used to armour weapons. In May 1944, following an Allied embargo, General Francisco Franco (shown in the doorway) agreed to limit how much wolfram Spain exported to Germany.

10 May 1944 — *Daily Express*

**'There 'e goes – says he's going to get this
ruddy invasion over, then get some leave.'**

Allied troops stationed on England's south coast awaited the order to invade France.

14 May 1944 — *Sunday Express*

The government of Vichy France – led by Pierre Laval (pictured) and Philippe Pétain – faced a wave of coordinated attacks by Resistance fighters, timed to coincide with the Allied invasion of Normandy.

8 June 1944 — *Daily Express*

'Himmel! Tourists!'

The Allied invasion of Northern France had begun on D-Day, 6 June 1944.

11 June 1944 — *Sunday Express*

'Didn't the B.B.C. say that he went back on Tuesday?'

Winston Churchill visited France on 13 June, venturing within three miles of the front line.

15 June 1944 — *Daily Express*

'Come in, Herr Rommel – come in and tell Uncle Adolf all about your West Wall.'

The Nazis' 'West Wall' of defences was designed to stop an Allied invasion in its tracks. Against the predictions of the German commander, Erwin Rommel, they were breached within hours of the invasion of Normandy.

18 June 1944 — *Sunday Express*

'It's ridiculous to say these flying bombs have affected people in ANY way.'

A week after the D-Day landings, Hitler unleashed his vengeance weapon: the V-1 bomb. At the height of the V-1 Blitz, 100 'Doodlebugs' – so-called because of their distinctive insect-like buzzing – were falling on London every day. The editor of the *Daily Express* wrote to Giles about this cartoon, 'Lots of people are saying your cartoon today is the funniest of the war. Congratulations on [a] brilliant achievement.'

11 July 1944 — *Daily Express*

'I alone decide the policy of Germany.' – Hitler, 1941

As Germany's defeat began to seem inevitable, Hitler's grip on power started to slip.
On 20 July, a military coup attempt had failed to overthrow the regime.

24 July 1944 — Daily Express

Warsaw Concerto

The 'Warsaw Concerto' was written by the composer Richard Addinsell to accompany the film *Dangerous Moonlight* (1941), which depicted the Polish battle against Nazi occupation. In August 1944, the Polish Resistance in Warsaw organised a major uprising which nearly toppled German rule in the city.

22 August 1944 — *Daily Express*

'If I am captured I would much prefer regular execution by beheading in the Tower of London to the farce of a noisy trial in Madison-square.' (Extract from Mussolini's Diaries, published in the North Italian Press)

Giles had a taste for absurdist humour: shown here, from left to right, are Goebbels, Hitler, Göring, Mussolini, Roosevelt, Stalin and Churchill.

27 August 1944 — *Sunday Express*

'They're taking all my toys!'

Under the leadership of generals Dwight Eisenhower and Bernard Montgomery, the Allied armies overran the Nazis' doodlebug launch sites.

7 September 1944 — *Daily Express*

'If my Mum could only see me now.'

Appearing under the headline 'Giles at the Battlefront', this cartoon of a British soldier capturing a Nazi was Giles's first from the front line. A caption explained: 'Giles, *Daily Express* cartoonist, flew to France days ago – the first cartoonist to be accredited as a war correspondent – to join the British armies and to draw the war as he sees it, in terms of his own famous, squat, and cheerful character, the Tommy of 1944.' The editorial promised that Giles would 'report the war in black-and-white in his own unmatchable way'.

3 October 1944 — *Daily Express*

'Massa's in the cold – cold ground'

With Germany too weak to protect its puppet state in North Italy, Mussolini's position as its figurehead became increasingly unstable. This cartoon refers to 'Massa's in de Cold Ground', a nineteenth-century minstrel song in which African-American slaves mourn the death of a 'kindly' slave-owner.

14 November 1944 — *Daily Express*

'O.K. – Let them in. But they're definitely the last.'

Rumours spread that senior Axis leaders had fled to their allies in Japan.

19 November 1944 — *Sunday Express*

'Stand down indeed. Serve 'em right if 'Itler was to drop
some ruddy paratroops over here this afternoon.'

On the day this cartoon was published, the Home Guard formally stood down
because the threat of invasion had ended.

3 December 1944 — *Sunday Express*

'Thought you were all nicely settled for the winter – didn't you?'

By December 1944, the Allied armies led by Bernard Montgomery had liberated northern France and were pushing east towards the Low Countries.

5 December 1944 — *Daily Express*

'All I say is, if you're going to take in everybody who resigns these days we're going to get mighty crowded.'

The imminent defeat of the Nazis caused a series of resignations by high-ranking Axis officials.

14 December 1944 — *Daily Express*

'Work it out, Len. Six sixteens is 96 – that's how many quids its
going to cost you to say "Merry Christmas" to this lot.'

A caption explained that Allied forces 'can be fined £16 for fraternising
with a German'.

17 December 1944 — *Sunday Express*

**'What's Rundstedt want to go counter-attacking for –
just when our retreat was going nicely.'**

In a last-ditch attempt to defeat the Allies, German forces led by Field Marshal Gerd
von Rundstedt began a final offensive in Belgium, France and Luxembourg.

21 December 1944 — *Daily Express*

**'Even if their War Crimes Commission does let us go free after the war, Himmler –
I can't imagine you settling down in a little grocery business or something.'**

In 1943, the Allies had created the War Crimes Commission to investigate German and
Japanese atrocities. Julius Streicher (right) would later be tried by the Commission, but
Himmler committed suicide in British custody before he could be charged.

16 January 1945 — *Daily Express*

'We are very fortunate, Herr Schmidt – the poor British Home Guard never had a chance to have a crack at the enemy.'

In October 1944, the increasingly desperate Nazi government had established the Volkssturm - a militia formed of men who had previously been thought too old to fight. It now became the primary force defending Germany.

23 January 1945 — *Daily Express*

'Hey you – how far is this Berchtesgaden?'

The Red Army liberated Poland and entered southeastern Germany, passing Berchtesgaden – famed as the location of Hitler's holiday home, the 'Eagle's Nest'.

'The only way you'll get a piece of Germany after the war will be to dig yourself one of those.'

The Allies were now firmly established on German soil in both the east and the west. Rumours continued to spread that Hitler and his senior advisers, including Goebbels and Göring, had fled Berlin.

18 February 1945 — *Sunday Express*

'Achtung! Which of you pigs blew that raspberry!'

The caption in the *Daily Express* explained, 'There have been signs of degeneration and slackness among German troops' along the French–German border.

25 February 1945 — *Daily Express*

'The oddest characters are coming in all the time in the ancient school buses, on which some wit has chalked "P.o.W. Express Service" . . .

. . . Becker was certainly co-operative when Giles took a snap of him sitting in his truck. The general stuck his chin out just a little bit further . . .

. . . and some soldiers chose security over their Fuehrer. They gave up so rapidly that before the end we were fighting boys of 15.'

This strip was drawn while Giles was in Bremen, to accompany captions written by the *Express* reporter Paul Holt. In April 1945, the commander of Nazi forces in Bremen, Fritz Becker, surrendered to the Allies and his soldiers were taken prisoner.

30 April 1945 — *Daily Express*

'Musso gorn, Goering gorn – you'll be in the cart when they've all gorn – won't 'ave nuffin to draw, will you?'

With Germany on the verge of defeat, Giles realised that all his favourite wartime characters were either dead or taken prisoner – and that a new range of characters would be needed. As Giles was uninterested in politics and politicians, he developed what he is now best remembered for: the Giles Family. Exactly a week after this cartoon was published, Germany surrendered.

1 May 1945 — *Daily Express*

**'There was only one man who entered Parliament
with good intentions – Guy Fawkes.'**

In Europe, the Second World War was over. The first general election since 1935 took place on 5 July. This cartoon perfectly sums up Giles's antipathy towards politics.

8 July 1945 — *Sunday Express*

'What's the betting that this Son of Heaven of ours ain't the Son of Heaven after all?'

Following the bombing of Hiroshima and Nagasaki, Japan unconditionally surrendered on 15 August, three days after this cartoon appeared. Emperor Hirohito was forced to retract the claim that he had been divinely appointed.

12 August 1945 — *Sunday Express*

'Be funny if the siren went now, wouldn't it?'

The British public took to the streets to celebrate victory over Japan on 15 August.

19 August 1945 — *Sunday Express*

**'These trials are a farce – WE never used to
waste time trying people.'**

In August, representatives of the Allied powers had agreed to try the
surviving Nazi leaders – including Göring, Hess and Speer – for war crimes.

2 September 1945 — *Sunday Express*

'The British are monsters . . . if they won the war they would turn us into a race of slaves.' (Extract from a Hitler speech, 1939.)

9 September 1945 — *Sunday Express*

'Must come strange to you, this idea of giving people a chance to defend themselves.'

Josef Kramer, Commandant of Bergen-Belsen concentration camp, was tried at Nuremburg in September 1945. Having witnessed the liberation of Bergen-Belsen first hand, Giles took a particularly keen personal interest in Kramer's trial.

19 September 1945 — *Daily Express*

'These demobs! If it's not Dunkirk it's Arnhem – if it's not Arnhem it's El Alamein.'

In September 1945, the new Labour government had announced its plan to demobilise the five million British troops stationed around the world.

7 October 1945 — *Sunday Express*

'Don't pull any of your parachute tricks this time, will you?'

Rudolf Hess, who had parachuted into Scotland in 1941 in an abortive attempt to make peace, was flown to Nuremberg on 8 October. He was one of the first German defendants to be charged as a war criminal.

9 October 1945 — *Daily Express*

Acknowledgements

I would like to thank the following for their support and assistance in putting this book together: Roger Hamlett, Alan Frame, Julie Dangoor, Elspeth Millar at the British Cartoon Archive, Alison Cullingford at the JB Priestley Library at the University of Bradford, Rebecca Harvey at Co-operative News, Natalie Jones at N&S Syndication and Licensing and Rowan Borchers at Penguin Random House.